Robots

Keith Gaines

The new teacher . . . . page 2
Things to do. . . . . page 22
The robot family. . . . . page 24
Things to do. . . . . page 31

The new teacher

Hello, Tim. Hello, Jack.

Hello, Miss Grey.

3

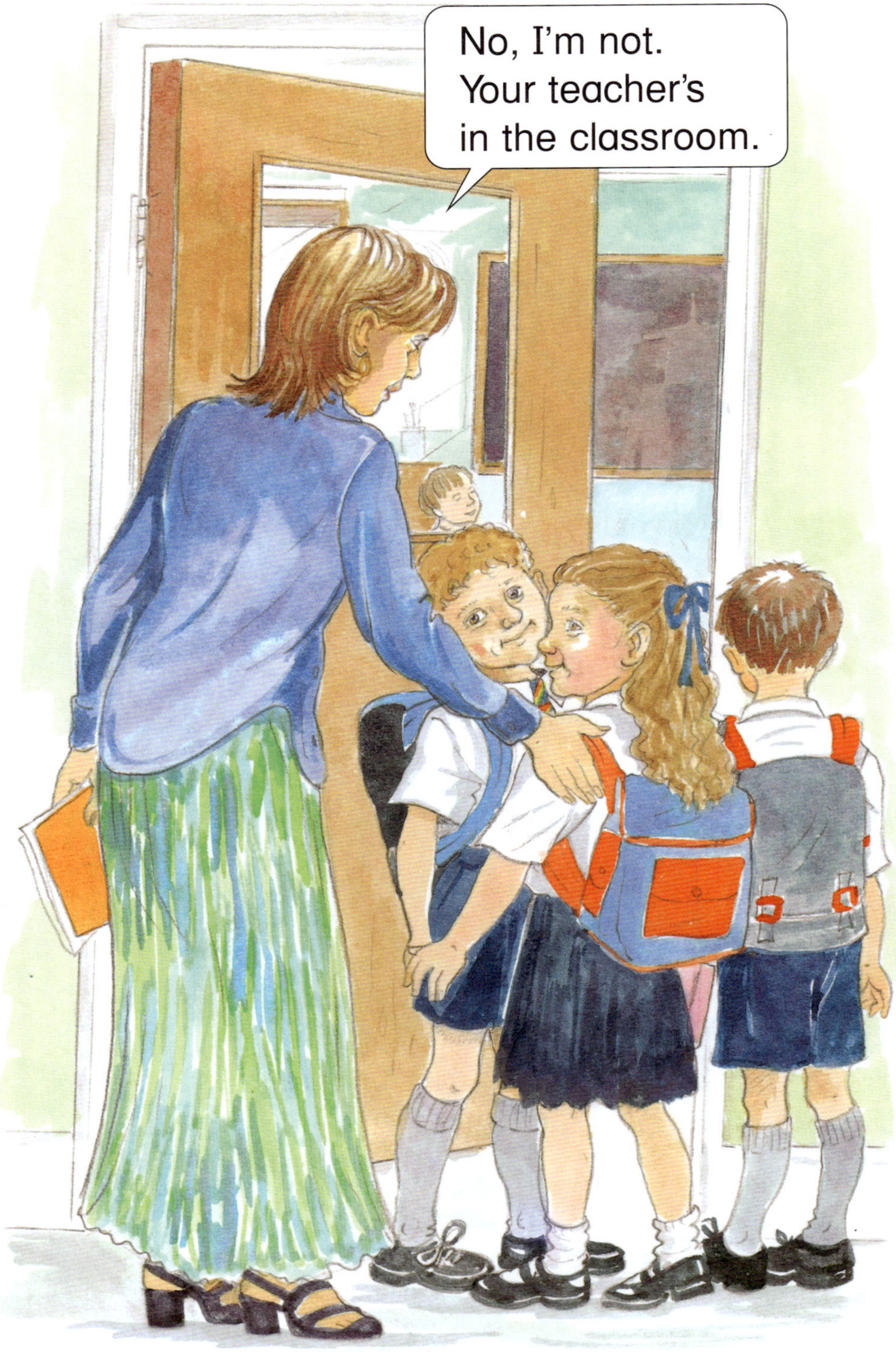
No, I'm not.
Your teacher's
in the classroom.

Look. Here's your teacher.

What's this?

What is it?

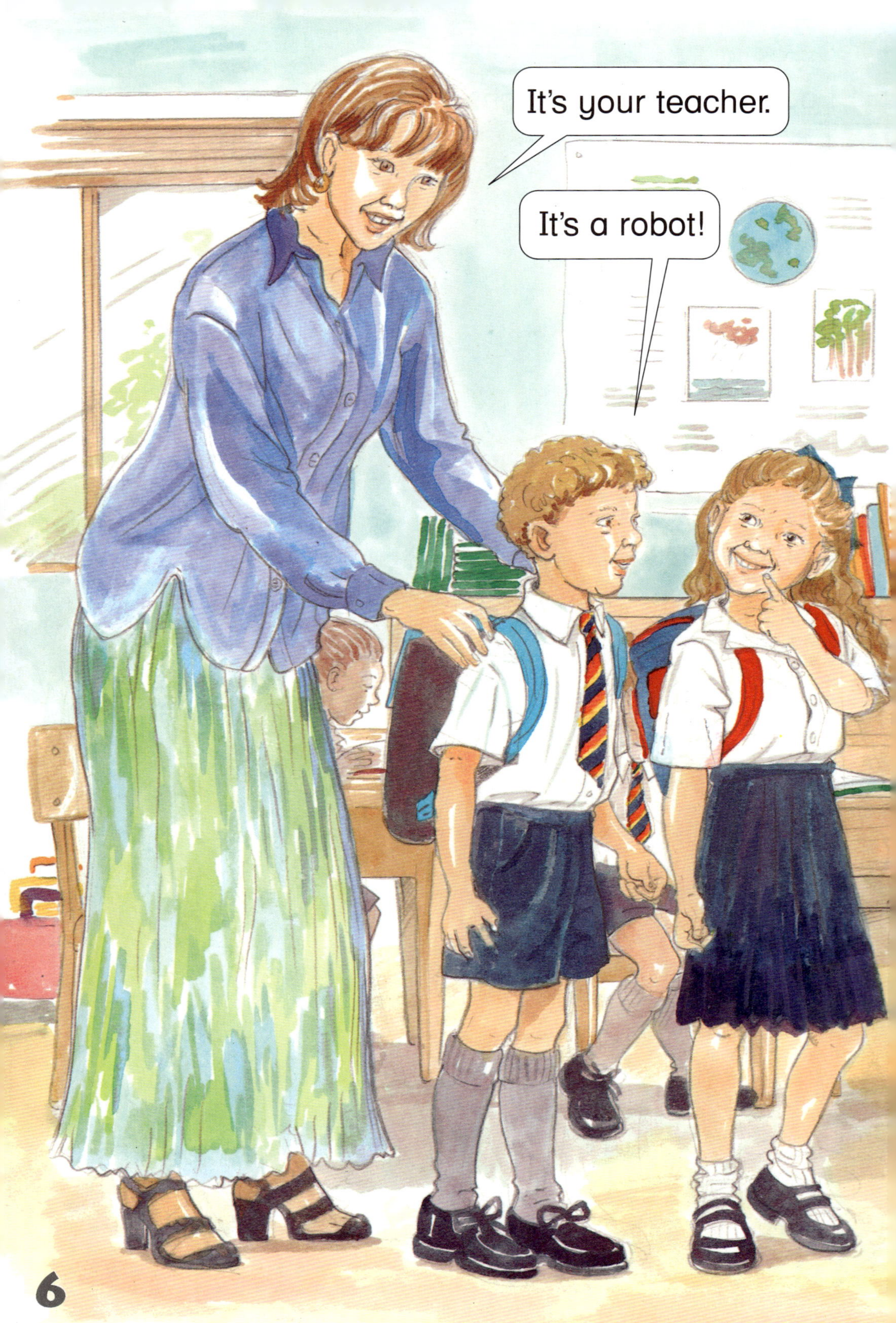
It's your teacher.
It's a robot!

7

How old are you, Jack?
I'm seven.
ROBOTEACHER

Hello, little boy.
My name is Roboteacher.
What's your name?
ROBOTEACHER
My name's Tim.

How old are you, Tim?
I'm six.

Is Jack your brother?
ROBOTEACHER
No, he's not my brother.

Is Jack your sister?
No, he's not my sister.

I'm not a girl.
No. He's a boy.
Jack's my friend.

Sit down, Jack.
Sit down, Tim.
You can sit next to Jack.
ROBOTEACHER

Hello, little girl.
My name is
Roboteacher.
What's your name?
My name's Sally.

Can you spell your
name please?
S – A – L – L – Y.
Thank you, Sally. Sit down.

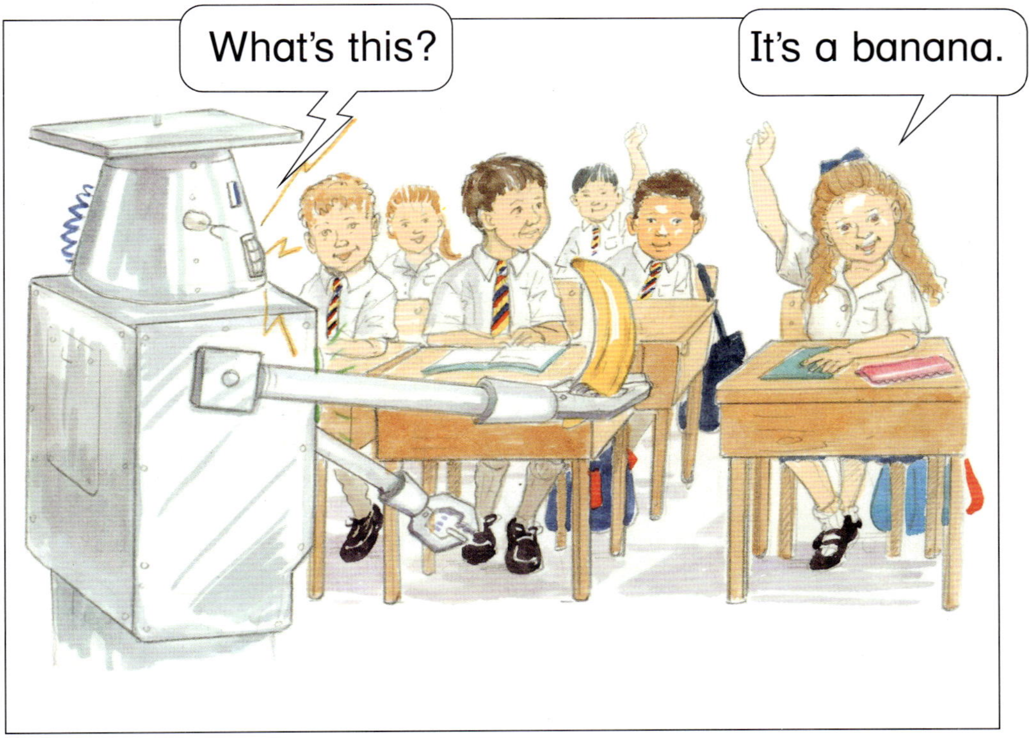
What's this?
It's a banana.

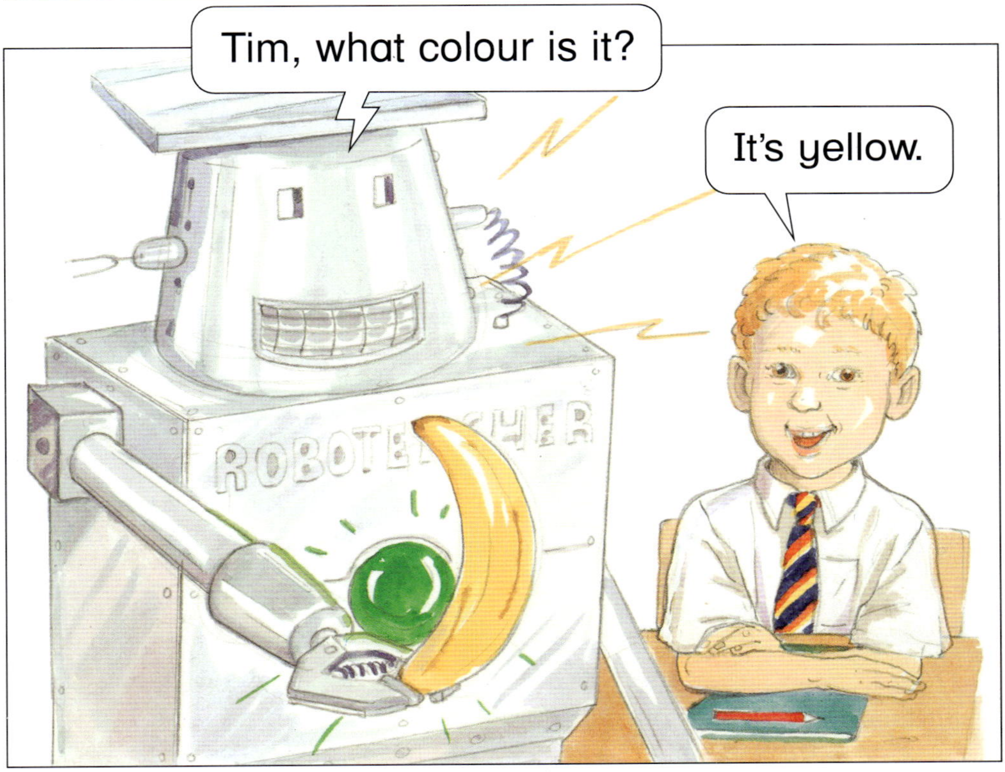
Tim, what colour is it?
It's yellow.

Jack, what is seven take away four?
Seven take away four is three.
7
-4
3
Yes it is.

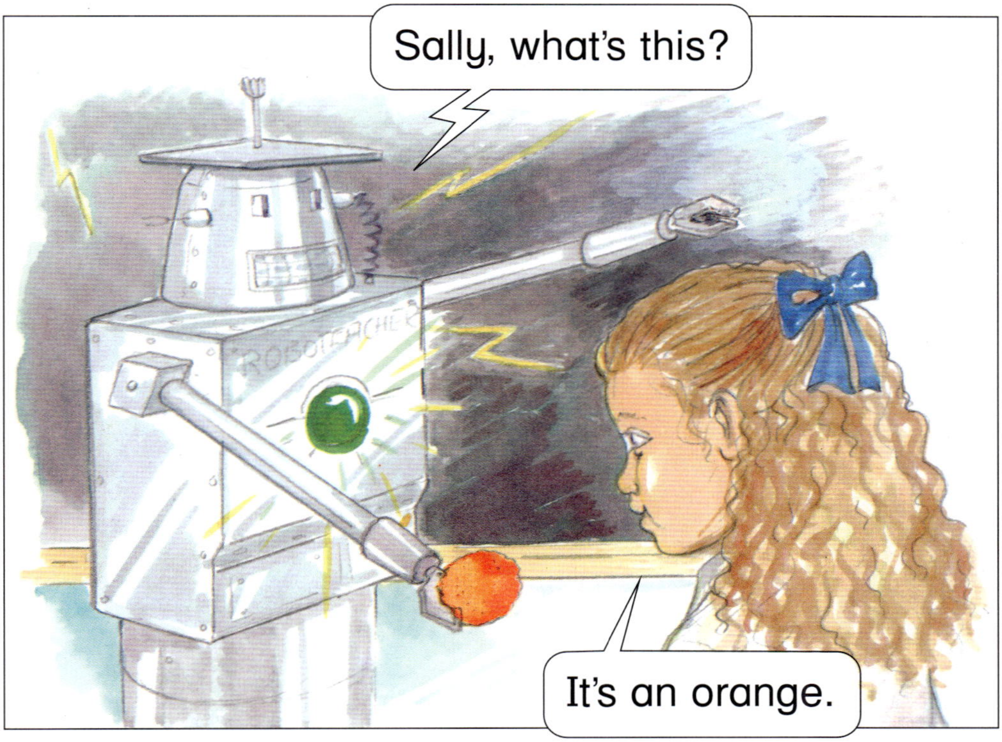
Sally, what's this?
It's an orange.

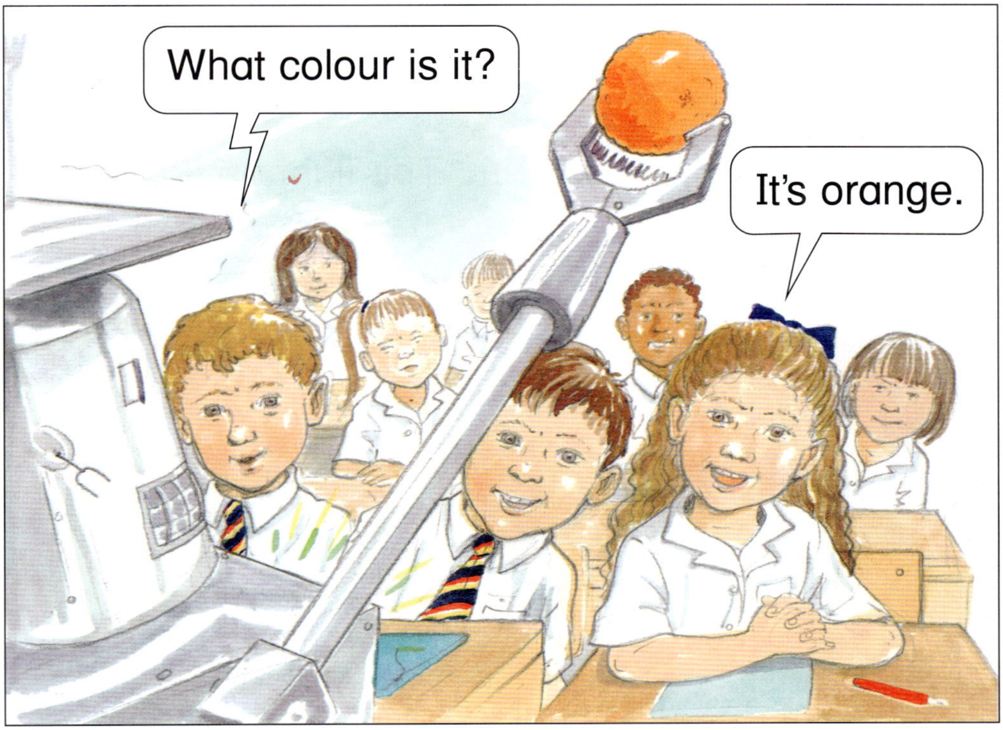
What colour is it?
It's orange.

No, it isn't. The orange is black.
ROBOTEACHER
Look, Tim. The light on the robot isn't green. It's yellow.

Tim, what is twelve take away two?
Twelve take away two is ten.
12
- 2
10

No. Twelve take away two is one.
ROBOTEACHER
No, it isn't!
12
- 2
10

Stand up! Sit down!
Stand up! Sit down!
Sit down! Stand up!

Look, the light on the robot isn't yellow. It's red!

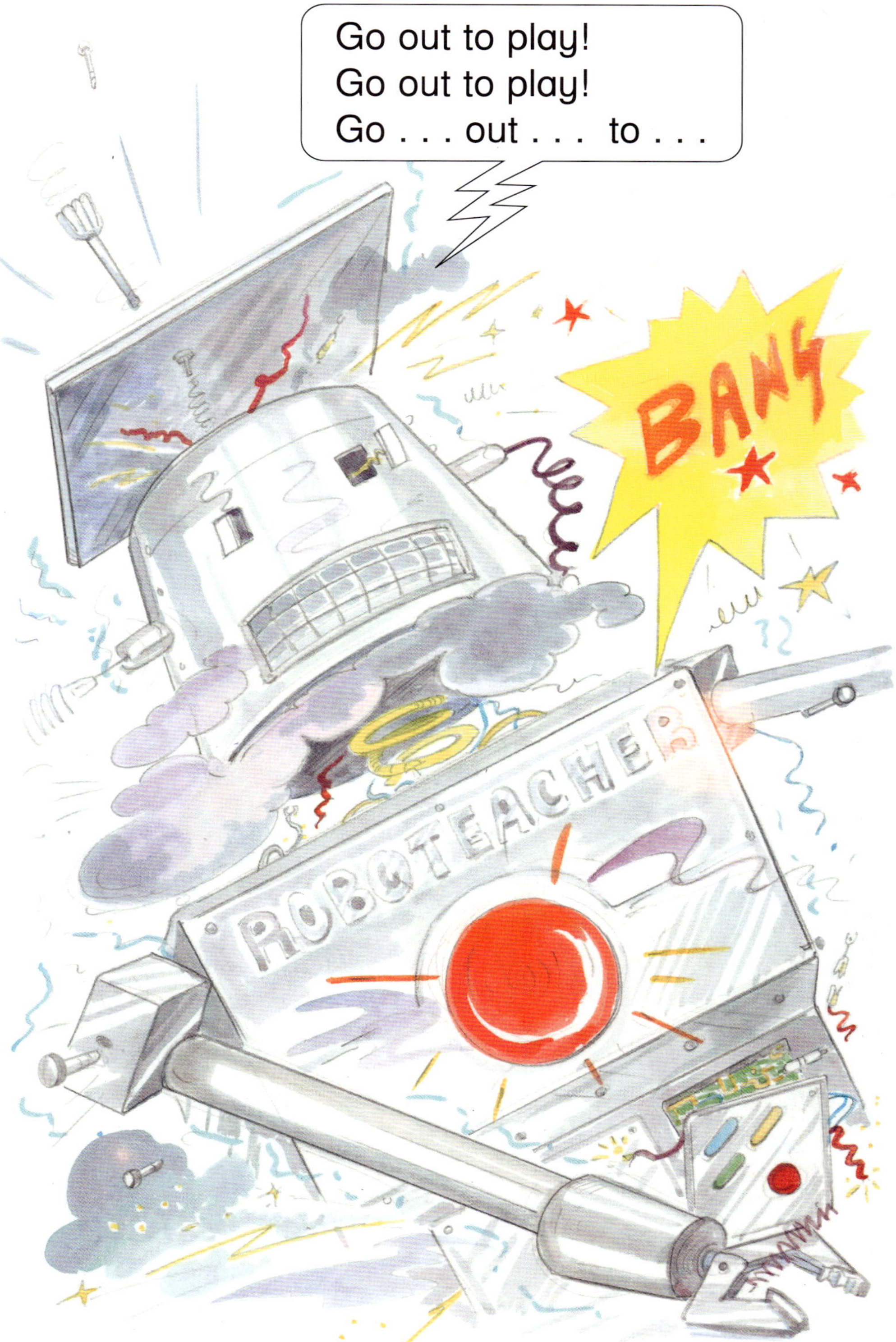
Go out to play!
Go out to play!
Go . . . out . . . to . . .
BANG
ROBOTEACHER

What's this? Where is Roboteacher?
He's under the table, Miss Grey.

I'm your teacher.
I'm happy.
I'm happy, too.
We have a teacher – not a robot!

Things to do

Here's Roboteacher.
Write the words in the boxes.

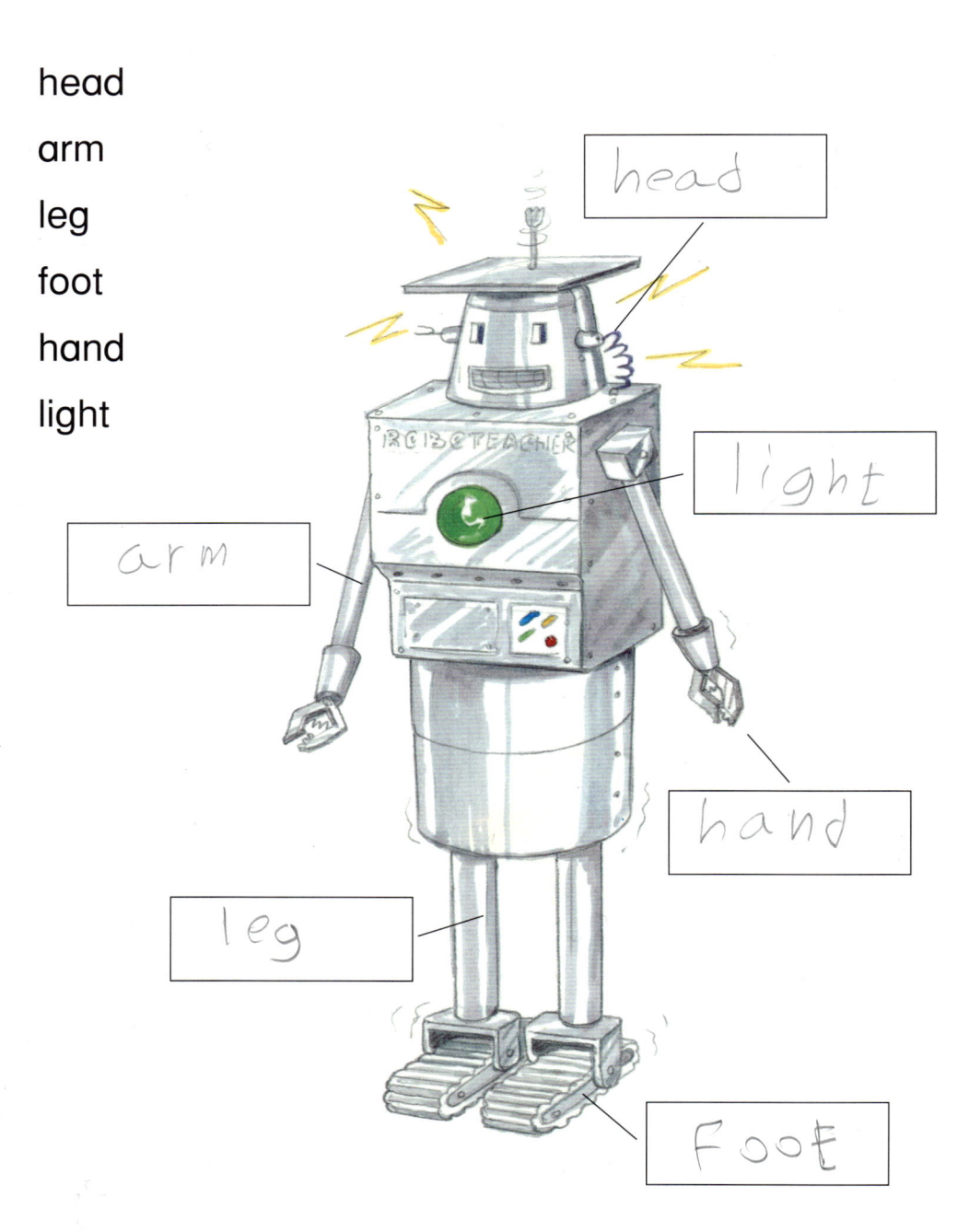

head

arm

leg

foot

hand

light

Handwritten labels on robot: head, light, arm, hand, leg, foot

Write the words ✏️

Hello, little boy. My name is Roboteacher.

What's your __name__?

My name's Jack.

How old are you?

I'm __seven__.

Hello, little boy. My name is Roboteacher.

What's __your__ name?

My name's __Tim__.

How __old__ are you?

I'm six.

The robot family

It is morning in the robot house . . .

robot flowers

robot hat

robot chair

robot table

Robot Grandmother
Robot Grandfather
lunch box
pencil case
robot sandwich
robot biscuits
robot teddy

25

Where's my pencil?
Where's my rubber?
Where's my ruler?
They are in the box on the table.
Thank you.
pencil case
lunch box

Where are my sandwiches?
They are in the box on the table.
Thank you.
pencil case

Goodbye!

Goodbye!

Goodbye!

robot duck

robot rabbit

happy robot teacher

19
−4

robot desk

lunch box

What's this? Where's my pencil?

lunch box

It's one o'clock.
It's time to eat my sandwiches.
pencil case

What's this?
Where are my sandwiches?
pencil case

Things to do

Write the words in the boxes.

a robot teddy   a robot hat
robot flowers   a robot sandwich
a robot table   robot biscuits

It's a robot Biscuits

It's a robot table

robot teddy bear

robot Flowers

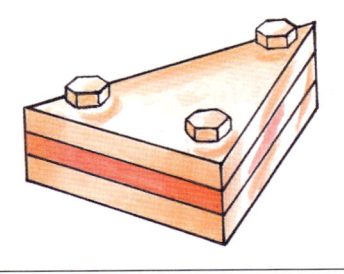

robot sandwich

robot hat

Macmillan Education
Between Towns Road, Oxford OX4 3PP
A division of Macmillan Publishers Limited
Companies and representatives throughout the world

www.macmillan-africa.com
www.macmillan-caribbean.com

ISBN : 978-0-333-67494-9

Text © Keith Gaines 1998
Design and illustration © Macmillan Publishers Limited 1998

First published 1998

All rights reserved; no part of this publication may be
reproduced, stored in a retrieval system, transmitted in any
form or by any means, electronic, mechanical, photocopying,
recording, or otherwise, without the prior written permission
of the publishers.

Illustrated by Lesley Smith/John Martin and Artists Limited and James Val

Cover illustration by Lesley Smith/John Martin and Artists Limited

Printed and bounded in Egypt by Sahara Printing Company

2009

15